Sam Chooses to be Brave

A Tent Camping Adventure

How to Enjoy This Book

Read this book just like any other! Snuggle under the covers or find your favorite sitting spot. Relax, open the book and enjoy the adventures of Sam! At the end of each chapter, you will be asked questions about the book. These questions are not hard. And some of them don't have right or wrong answers. The goal of this book is to help you think while you read. Active reading is asking questions and thinking about the book while you read. This helps you remember what you read. And remembering makes you a better reader!

Chapter One

Sam's stomach flipped as their car pulled into Cades Cove Campground. The dark woods of the Great Smoky Mountains National Park surrounded him on either side.

"The sun's going down already," he said. Mom nodded as she looked for their site. "It does get dark early now. But there might still be time to explore."

No way, thought Sam. Exploring in the dark was the last thing he wanted to do.

Daniel, who was eleven and knew everything, contorted his face into a scary shape. He leaned over to whisper, "Hope we get in the tent before *they* come out!"

Sam rolled his eyes, but turned away to hide the worried look on his face. It was hard to be eight and not exactly sure if all the scary things your older brother said were true or not. A large dark image danced into his mind, but he squeezed his eyes shut and willed it away. They had been traveling for two weeks now on an epic camping adventure, working their way from Arizona to Tennessee and tent camping along the way. A definite plus to homeschooling was you could camp even after school started. But ever since Daniel told Sam about the kid-eating bears of the Great Smoky Mountains, Sam felt unsure about the whole thing.

Mom pulled the car into lot thirteen. "Here we are!" she cheered.

Sam gave a weak smile.

After hauling out the gear, Mom lit the green lantern and hung it from the pole near the picnic table. A circle of light poured over the campsite. Sam breathed a sigh of relief and positioned himself in the middle of it. Here he was safe. Outside of this, he wasn't so sure.

Daniel grabbed him from behind and he screamed.

"Cut it out!" Sam yelled.

Mom looked up from unfolding the tent. "Daniel, stop messing with him. Go and find some sticks for the hotdogs."

Daniel stepped back into the darkness, giving a spooky smile as he disappeared into the night.

After dinner they settled into the blue tent. "Hey kid," Mom said as she leaned in to kiss him goodnight. "You okay?"

Sam nodded.

"You look a little worried."

Daniel made a mocking face. "Are you scared?"

"No!" Sam said.

Mom frowned. "Well I don't know what is going on, but if someone is trying to scare you..." she glanced at Daniel, "just remember, don't believe everything you hear."

Sam smiled. "Okay," he said.

But as soon as Mom went into her room of the tent, Daniel leaned over.

"But believe this... they are everywhere, and they're watching!"

Sam rolled over in his bag so Daniel couldn't see his face. Sam knew his brother was full of baloney. But then again...

The moon rose up into the sky. Sam looked at his brother, fast asleep and probably dreaming about marshmallows. Sam was wide awake. He stared at the sky through the mesh tent ceiling.

Suddenly he heard something crunching through the leaves on the side of the tent. Something was moving through the brush. Sam pulled the sleeping bag tight to his neck. Every inch of his body went stiff.

The sounds grew closer.

His mind swirled around and made him dizzy. The crunch crunch of the footsteps grew louder. Sam stared at the tent door. Only one little zipper stood between him and the beast he was sure stood outside the door. He could almost hear it breathing! There *are* bears here, Sam thought. Daniel was right!

Then Sam heard a lady's voice calling someone. Sam sat up fast. If a lady was out there she would get eaten for sure! He forced himself to the window flap. If it *was* a bear, maybe he could yell and scare it away. But he couldn't make himself pull the flap open. He took a breath and counted, "1... 2... 3," and flung it up. There it was! He was staring right into its face!

Chapter One Questions:

-    What do you think is outside the tent?

_____

-    What are the names of the two brothers?

_____

-    What animal is Sam most afraid to meet in the woods?

_____

Chapter Two

There it was, the biggest white poodle Sam had ever seen. He sighed with relief. This was definitely not a bear! The poodle wore a glittery pink t-shirt. A lady in ice cream cone pajama pants ran up to his tent out of breath.

"Maddie Grace, get over here," she hissed.

The poodle licked the mesh tent window, then trotted off with its owner.

Sam fell back onto his silky sleeping bag. He felt like he had looked death in the eye, even though he was pretty sure death didn't wear a pink glittery outfit. He crawled into his bag and fell right asleep.

The next morning Sam woke up to the heavenly smells of bacon. Stepping out of the tent, the campground now looked sunny and cheerful. It sat right on the edge of a lake, glittering bright blue in the early sun. His site was part of a circle of campgrounds. Each full with another family camping in tents or campers.

Sam stretched and Mom pulled him into a hug.

"Good morning, honey bunny," she said.

Sam waved her away, hoping the other campers didn't hear. "Where's the bathroom?" he yawned.

Mom pointed to a brown building across the gravel road. It stood next to a playground and a field.

At breakfast, Daniel and Sam wolfed down their bacon, eggs and orange juice. They laughed about how Mom always burned the bacon.

Afterwards they cleaned up and Mom gathered the leftovers into the cooler.

"Daniel, stick this back in the car, please," Mom said.

Sam cocked his head. "Why? We're not leaving. Let's just leave it here."

"Can't," Mom said, wiping the plastic tablecloth. "We're in Bear Country now." She pointed to a sign.

Sam gulped and read it. It said:

"Be Bear Aware! Food and Odors Attract Bears."

Sam felt queasy. He glanced at his brother who gave him a knowing look.

"But there aren't really a lot around here, right?" He asked hopefully.

Mom dried off the cast iron pan. "Actually, there are a lot of Black bears in the Smokies. So maybe we'll get lucky and see one." She turned back to her work.

"Yeah, maybe," Sam muttered. The tight feeling in his stomach was coming back again.

Sam drug his feet as he carried the trash to the funny green can. It almost looked like a giant mailbox, only he was going to open the door and mail his garbage. This can was designed to keep wildlife from getting into the trash for food. It was another sign bears were around.

He slid the trash in, as a purple ball bounced past his feet. A girl in a purple baseball cap ran up and grabbed it.

"Hey!" she said.

"Hey," said Sam.

"I'm Beatrice," said the girl, putting the ball on her hip.

"I'm Sam."

"You like worms?" Beatrice said. "Cause I know a good place where there are a whole bunch."

Sam thought about it. He couldn't say he *liked* worms, but he liked them better than hanging out with Daniel. "Yeah, I guess," he said.

"Oh good!" said Beatrice, as she ran off toward the trees on the far side of the campground circle. "Follow me," she called back, running to the trail that went into the woods. Sam gulped. He wasn't good at math but he knew one simple fact: woods equaled bears.

Chapter Two Questions:

- What does Sam think is in the woods?

_____

- What is the name of Sam's new friend, the girl in the purple baseball cap?

_____

- Why is Daniel told to put the leftovers back in the car?

_____

Chapter Three

Sam watched Beatrice disappear into the woods. He took a breath. He decided to just go to the edge and see what it was like. After a quick check-in with Mom, he followed after Beatrice.

Sam stopped just inside the trees. Immediately it felt dark and cool. Almost like a cave, he thought. Almost like a *bear* cave. Sam's eyes darted all around as his heart beat fast.

Beatrice doubled back on the trail. "It's just up here," she called. "Come on!"

Sam bit his lip and took a step further in, but stopped. Surely bears, kid-eating bears, wouldn't hang around this close to the campground, would they? Or maybe kid-eating bears were smart and knew this was exactly the place to find lunch. He took another step, the gravel on the trail crunching under his sneakers. But he couldn't go any further.

Beatrice ran up to meet him. "Hey, what's up?" she said.

Sam stiffened. "Nothing, I just," he looked all around for an excuse to tell Beatrice, anything but the fact that he was afraid. He spotted a small pine sapling growing up in the path. "I think that might be poison ivy?" he said, pointing.

Beatrice looked at the plant then looked at him like he was crazy. "Where are you *from*?" she said.

"Arizona," Sam said sheepishly. "We're on a road trip."

Beatrice nodded. "Well, I'm from here. And let me tell you, that is not poison ivy. It has three leaves and doesn't look at all like that."

Sam nodded. He felt so dumb. He was a boy scout. He *knew* that wasn't poison ivy! But how do you say to a kid you just met, "Hey, I'm afraid a bear might eat me if I go in the woods because my mean brother told me a scary story?" You don't say that. Instead, you make yourself look like a world class dummy.

Then suddenly Sam heard a rustling further up the path. This time he knew it wasn't Maddie Grace the poodle, as he had passed her on his way to the trail.

Beatrice looked back up the path. "Uh, what was that?"

Realizing she heard it too made Sam worry more. Every voice in him was yelling, "It's a bear, run!"

But his body wouldn't move.

The rustling grew louder. Something was coming up ahead for sure. Beatrice stepped forward toward it.

"No stop!" Sam whispered.

Beatrice ignored him. "Come on," she said back. "I think I know what it is."

Yeah, I do too, thought Sam. But he couldn't let Beatrice meet a kid-eating bear on her own. He forced his legs to walk.

Then, the creature bounded out right in front of them!

Chapter Three Questions:

- Why does Sam say he sees poison ivy?

_____

- What kind of animals live in the woods? What kind of animal do you think is right in front of Sam and Beatrice?

_____

- Where did Sam say he is from?

_____

Chapter Four

The creature bounded at them, then froze. Sam breathed a sigh of relief. It was a deer.

Beatrice laughed, as the deer leapt off into the brush.

"I thought it was a deer," she said. "I was hoping we could get closer before it ran off."

Sam smiled weakly. He felt like he might pass out.

Beatrice seemed to notice. "Hey, let's forget about the worms and go get some juice boxes at my camp."

Sam nodded. Maybe juice could help his knees stop shaking so hard.

The two kids sat on the swings of the playground sipping the last of their juice. Sam felt much better in the sunshine.

"I think we should go to the creek," Beatrice said.

Sam nodded. Swimming sounded wonderful.

Beatrice jumped up. "Let's race to see who gets changed first. Go!" She darted off toward her camper.

Sam didn't feel like racing, but he still tried to hurry. Beatrice was fun, but he couldn't wait until they would leave this place. At least he was fairly sure bears would avoid the loud splashing and screaming coming from the creek. It seemed like every kid in the campground must be there.

At the creek, Daniel and two red-haired older boys splashed and dunked each other.

Sam and Beatrice rolled her giant black innertube toward the water, passing a toddler playing on the edge.

"Let's see if we can float on it and dangle our feet in the middle," Sam suggested.

Beatrice loved the idea. They pushed the large donut into the cool water.

Sam, pretty sure that bears didn't scuba dive, felt safe here. He and Beatrice looked down through the middle of the innertube as fish swam under their feet.

Daniel splashed over. "Hey Sam, I wondered where you were. Where'd you get that tire?"

"Hey," said Sam. "It's hers. This is Beatrice."

Daniel held onto the edge. "Cool."

Suddenly Sam felt something pinch his leg. "Hey!" he said, jerking it out of the water. "What was that?" He rubbed his leg.

"What?" said Beatrice, trying to steady the float in the water.

Sam looked into the dark blue water. "Something pinched me."

Daniel looked concerned. "Or bit you!"

Beatrice searched the water below. "Maybe a fish?"

Daniel shook his head. "Maybe, but it could've been a snake. They have water snakes here, and I saw one back by those trees. I'm outta here!" He splashed Sam as he swam back to his new friends.

Sam's face grew pale. He stared at his leg for bite marks. He couldn't see any, but still....

Beatrice stared at his leg. "I don't think it was a snake. I bet Daniel pinched you." She frowned. "He's just messing with you."

Sam nodded uneasily. "Yeah, maybe." He knew that was probably right. Daniel had been messing with him on this whole trip. But it was hard to know what to believe. Suddenly he didn't feel much like swimming, he looked toward the snake-free shore. "I think my Mom might need me. I'm going to go."

Beatrice frowned. "You sure?"

"Yeah," Sam said, climbing out of the tube.

Sam walked out of the water feeling a million pounds and weighed down by it all. He knew it probably wasn't a snake, but he couldn't be sure. Just like he couldn't be sure that bears wouldn't eat him. He slogged back to camp and collapsed into the hammock. The sounds of kids, carefree kids playing at the creek, drifted over to him. They were kids who were brave. Kids who weren't him.

Chapter Four Questions:

- Did Daniel pinch Sam or did a snake bite him?

_____

- Can you think of a time you weren't sure if someone was telling you the truth?

_____

- Why did Sam initially want to go into the water?

_____

Chapter Five

After lunch, Sam wandered over to the playground.

Beatrice ran up. "Hey! There you are! Some kids are playing pirates at the playground. Do you want to be part of the Navy or a Pirate? I'm Navy," she said, standing tall with pride.

"Uh, Navy?" Sam said.

Beatrice grabbed his arm. "Well come on then! They are about to capture Barbados!"

After all the pirates were captured, walked off the plank, and the oceans safe again for law-abiding ships, Sam and Beatrice grew hungry. They pillaged her cooler for popsicles and sat in the low branches of an Oak tree. Acorn caps littered the ground below.

Sam slurped his quickly melting popsicle and smiled. But then he remembered the night was coming on before long. Sam pictured a giant black bear, its fangs dripping with drool as it crept toward his tent.

He shivered.

Beatrice stared at him. "You seem worried."

Sam shook his head. "Huh? No... no."

"You sure?" Beatrice asked.

Sam tried to smile. "Yeah! Why would I be worried?" He gave a little laugh, then stared at his popsicle. Was Beatrice buying it? He couldn't tell.

Beatrice cocked her head to the side. "You aren't very good at lying," she said.

Nope, thought Sam. She wasn't buying any of it.

He traced the bark on the tree limb. Should he just tell her? Should he tell her he was scared of being rolled up in his tent like a giant burrito and eaten by a bear? Would she laugh? Would she tell all the other kids he was a big chicken?

He looked up at her expecting her to have the mean look Daniel had when he teased him. But instead, Beatrice looked concerned. She looked like a friend.

Sam took a big breath.

Beatrice smiled. "Y'know, I had to go to a whole new school last year, in the middle of the year." She sighed. "It was pretty bad. I didn't know anybody and all the kids knew each other. Every Monday morning I felt pretty scared to go."

Sam looked at her. For the first time, he considered that maybe Beatrice felt afraid too sometimes.

Beatrice bit her lip. "It was hard to get up and go. But my Mom said, 'Girl, being brave doesn't mean you aren't afraid.' She said, 'Being brave is choosing to do what you need to do anyways, even if you're afraid. That's being brave.'"

Sam looked at his sneakers. Could *he* choose to be brave? He wasn't sure.

"And she also said I *had* to go," Beatrice laughed, "so I went."

Sam looked at her hopefully. "And you weren't scared anymore?"

Beatrice shook her head. "Are you crazy? I was terrified!" She swung her legs over the thick branch and jumped down. "But I did it anyway. And it got better."

She smiled.

Sam smiled back. He was just about to tell her about his bear fear, when Beatrice's mom called her.

"Ooh, I better go," she said. "I have some chores. But I'll see you on the night hike!" She said running off.

Sam almost fell off the branch. "The what?!" he yelled after her, but she was too far away to hear.

Sam ran back to his campsite with his mind swirling. There was no way he was going on any night hike, that was for sure!

But as he got to his site, his mom was waving goodbye to the park ranger.

"Who was that?" Sam asked out of breath.

Mom smiled. "Hey sweetie! That was Park Ranger Tim. He just invited us to the night hike tonight. Won't that be cool!"

Sam nearly fell over as Mom turned back to the grill to light the charcoal for dinner.

He was dizzy. A night hike! A night hike! That was all he could think. He would be eaten by a bear for sure, and it was happening tonight!

Chapter Five Questions:

-       Why is Sam afraid of going on the night hike?

_____

-       Think about Beatrice's story about going to a new school. Have you ever chosen to be brave? Did choosing to be brave mean you weren't afraid anymore?

_____

-       Is Beatrice a good friend or a bad friend?

_____

Chapter Six

At dinner Sam only nibbled half a burger because it was hard to eat when you knew you were going to die.

It was one hour to the night hike. They would be meeting at the Anthony Creek Trailhead. The trail crossed a stream several times. Bears liked streams, Sam thought. He lay on his sleeping bag alone in the tent.

He lay as still as he could be. He was practicing. Maybe if he pretended to be dead when he saw a bear it would leave him alone and go for some other kid. He hated to do it, but this was survival. He would have to tell Beatrice what to do also.

But everytime he thought he looked really dead, a fly would tickle his nose or a mosquito would buzz in his ear and he would blow it. He would just have to keep at it.

Daniel unzipped the tent. "What are you doing?" he asked. "You look like you're dead." He fell into the tent and plopped down on his bag.

Sam ignored him.

Daniel flipped over. "It's too hot, and I'm bored."

Sam could feel him watching him. He opened his eyes.

"Hey, I never told you the end of my story,"

Daniel said.

Sam groaned.

"There's another part," Daniel said.

Oh no, thought Sam.

Daniel began. "So the kids that escaped the first time from the bear were the Johnson twins."

Sam tried to shut his ears, but he couldn't. "And the bear was after them. He crept through the dark woods, watching them..."

Sam couldn't take it. He jumped up. "I *don't* want to hear this!" he yelled.

Daniel laughed. "It's not even that scary! Don't be a wimp."

Sam was tired. Tired of his brother pushing and poking him, making him feel afraid, making him feel like a coward. He balled his hands into two hard fists.

"I'm not a wimp," he growled as a hot anger grew in his chest. He wanted to punch his brother through the tent wall.

"I can't believe you're afraid of bears," Daniel said. "You know they can tell that, right? The chicken-hearted kid is the one they always get first."

That was it! Sam charged at his brother, but Daniel jumped back. Sam was so mad he was crying. His face was red.

"You are the biggest jerk!" Sam yelled, and tore past his brother out of the tent.

"Sam" Mom called after him, but he just kept running.

He ran and ran until he was past the bathrooms, and the playground, and the picnic pavilion. He ran until he stopped in a completely different part of the campground. He wiped his runny nose and wet face on his shirt and climbed under an empty picnic table. He was mad, and sad, and everything, all at once. He would show Daniel. He *would* be brave! He would choose it, like Beatrice said, and he would go on that night hike if it was the last thing he did. And the odds were it probably would be. But if Sam was going to be eaten by a bear that night, he would be the bravest kid who ever was eaten in the history of the world.

Chapter Six Questions:

-       Why is Daniel telling Sam the scary story? Is he being nice or being mean?

_____

-       What do you do when you are angry, sad and mad all at the same time?

_____

-       Are you afraid of bears? What sorts of things make you feel scared?

_____

Chapter Seven

On the way to the trail head, Sam breathed deeply as he took big steps. He was on a mission: to die with bravery. Daniel looked humbled as Mom was pretty mad to find out how much he had been pestering Sam.

Daniel came up next to him. "Hey man," he said. "I guess I was kind of taking it too far."
Sam nodded but didn't look at him. This wasn't about Daniel anymore. This was about himself and being brave.

The sun was setting and Sam clutched his flashlight. He felt a small flicker of relief when Beatrice waved and ran over.

"Hey!" she said. "This is going to be so cool!"

Sam bit his lip and nodded.

Park Ranger Tim gathered everyone at the trailhead. "Okay people, I'm glad everyone could come! The important thing will be to stay together. We are bound to see some really interesting wildlife if we look closely. We may see bats, opossums, possibly a fox if we're lucky. It's quite possible to see Barred Owls. And don't forget to look down for toads and sometimes mice. We may find a few deer. I hope you'll see the woods are full of life."

Sam felt a moment of excitement at the mention of the animals, but then he remembered he was scared. A four-year old in bright orange shorts asked the question he was wondering.

"What about bears?" the boy said.

Park Ranger Tim laughed. "Well, our black bears aren't regular guests on this hike, sorry. They don't much like a big crowd like ours, although they are active in the early morning or late evening. But I haven't seen any lately on this side of the forest, so seeing one isn't very likely."

A few kids groaned, but Sam felt hope. Was it possible he might not die? It was promising. He relaxed his shoulders a little as the group set off into the woods.

Sam turned on his flashlight and shone it into the dark woods. A shiver ran up his spine. He jumped when Beatrice tapped his shoulder.

"Hey Sam, isn't this great!" she said.

Sam nodded weakly.

The group started off on the trail. Sam tried to remember to breathe and he focused on his feet hitting the gravelly path.

Daniel pushed past him with the two boys from the lake. "I hope we see some snakes," he heard him say.

Sam just hoped Beatrice was a fast runner when the bear came. He swallowed and his throat felt dry. I can choose to be brave, he said to himself. I can choose to be brave. He wasn't sure he could believe that, but he was trying.

Suddenly the group stopped.

"If you look to your left," said Park Ranger Tim, pointing to a tall pine tree, "you will see an eagle's nest." Everyone pointed their flashlights into the tree. A grumpy eagle peered over the edge and stared at them.

Mom smiled at Sam. Sam tried his best to smile back. He walked faster to avoid showing her he was not enjoying himself. Before he knew it, he was at the front of the group, right behind the park ranger and Beatrice, who was eager to learn all she could.

"The stream is just up here," said Park Ranger Tim. "Don't slip as we cross on the large flat rocks."

Daniel came up next to him as they turned the corner. "I hope we don't fall in and. . . ." Daniel froze.

"What is it?" said Sam.

But Daniel didn't answer. He looked like he'd seen a ghost!

Sam looked over to what his brother was staring at. He saw it just as Park Ranger Tim did.

Drinking at the stream, unaware he had an audience, was a real live Black Bear!

Chapter Seven Questions:

-      Why does Sam hope Beatrice is a fast runner? Is Sam a good or bad friend to Beatrice?

_____

-      Would you be scared to go on a night hike? Or excited? Or both?

_____

-      Do you think the Park Ranger was telling the truth about not expecting to see a bear? What's the difference between telling a lie and just not being right about something?

_____

Chapter Eight

Park ranger Tim put his hand up to stop the group. "Everyone remain calm," he whispered, as the bear looked up startled by the people staring at him.

Sam knew he should be scared. He knew he should be terrified! This was a real bear, and it was less than twenty feet in front of him!

But this bear looked nothing like the kid-eating bear of Daniel's stories. This bear was huge, fuzzy, and actually pretty cool.

The weird thing was the bear looked scared of *them*! His giant tongue licked the water off his lips. He snorted out a loud breath.

Park Ranger Tim reached to the can of bear spray on his belt, in case the bear decided to come closer. But, it turned out, the bear didn't want a run in with thirty-two campers and flashlights and bear spray. He turned to the side and shuffled off into the dark trees.

Beatrice grabbed Sam's arm. "This is amazing!" she whispered.

Sam nodded, watching the last bit of the bear disappear from view. It *was* amazing. Sam turned to his brother, but was surprised to find Daniel frozen in fear, his knees shaking, unable to speak. He's terrified!, Sam thought. He's been teasing me this whole time, and he's terrified!

Sam shook his head in disbelief. He could really let him have it, and he deserved all the teasing he would get!

But then Sam looked at his brother again and felt something else. Sam knew what it was like to be scared and he didn't really want to tease him after all. Sam patted Daniel on the back. "Come on," he said. "It's gone now."

Park ranger Tim gathered the group close keeping an eye on where the bear had been. "Well that was something," he said, letting out a breath.

Everyone agreed. Mom squeezed up next to Sam and Daniel.

"But unfortunately, we'll need to head back now."

A few people groaned.

"That's our policy," Park Ranger Tim went on. "If we have a bear sighting, we head back to camp."

Mom squeezed her kids. "Wasn't that exciting!"

Daniel smiled weakly, still looking a little queasy, but Sam grinned.

"It was the best!" he said.

Walking back on the trail felt like walking on the moon. Sam was in a whole new world of sounds and smells and sights. A bat zoomed just over his head across the path. And a fat toad jumped out of his way.

Sam wanted to laugh and jump for joy! He had chosen to be brave, and in the end, he didn't even need to be brave after all. Sam knew bears were wild animals and still different from teddy bears, but now he knew they weren't monsters and they weren't after him or other kids. All the fears and worries of the past days melted away. He was free.

That night in his tent, listening to Daniel snoring and Maddie Grace the poodle rustling through the leaves outside his tent, Sam couldn't wait for the next day to begin. He would swim, then play in the woods with Beatrice, then swim again. And nothing would stop him.

Chapter Eight Questions:

- Why do you think Daniel teased Sam so bad about bears?

_____

- Have you ever chosen to be brave like Sam? Did it feel just as free when you did the scary thing?

_____

- What do you think the bear was thinking when he saw the group of kids on the night hike?

_____

Congratulations! You finished a whole chapter book!

How did you like this story of Sam's adventure? Would you like a friend like Beatrice? You deserve a pat on the back for being a great reader! We have more books about Sam's adventures!

We've included this section for you to write anything you want about this book. How did this story make you feel? Do you wish something happened differently? Do you want to go on a tent camping adventure?

Made in the USA
Las Vegas, NV
21 July 2021